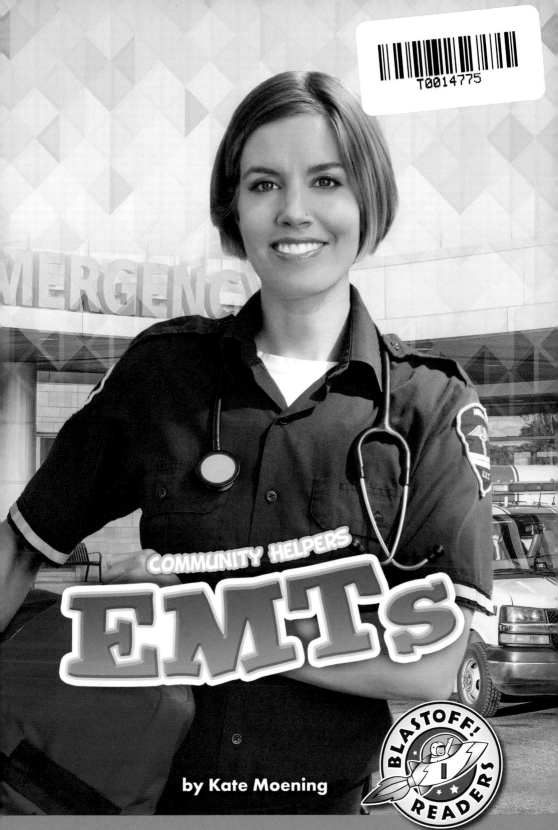

COMMUNITY HELPERS

EMTs

by Kate Moening

BLASTOFF! READERS

BELLWETHER MEDIA • MINNEAPOLIS, MN

Blastoff! Readers are carefully developed by literacy experts to build reading stamina and move students toward fluency by combining standards-based content with developmentally appropriate text.

Level 1 provides the most support through repetition of high-frequency words, light text, predictable sentence patterns, and strong visual support.

Level 2 offers early readers a bit more challenge through varied sentences, increased text load, and text-supportive special features.

Level 3 advances early-fluent readers toward fluency through increased text load, less reliance on photos, advancing concepts, longer sentences, and more complex special features.

★ **Blastoff! Universe**

Reading Level

Grade **K**

Grades **1-3**

Grade **4**

This edition first published in 2021 by Bellwether Media, Inc.

No part of this publication may be reproduced in whole or in part without written permission of the publisher. For information regarding permission, write to Bellwether Media, Inc., Attention: Permissions Department, 6012 Blue Circle Drive, Minnetonka, MN 55343.

Library of Congress Cataloging-in-Publication Data

Names: Moening, Kate, author.
Title: EMTs / Kate Moening.
Description: Minneapolis, MN : Bellwether Media, Inc., 2021. | Series: Blastoff! readers: Community helpers | Includes bibliographical references and index. | Audience: Ages 5-8 | Audience: Grades K-1 | Summary: "Developed by literacy experts for students in kindergarten through grade three, this book introduces EMTs to young readers through leveled text and related photos"–Provided by publisher.
Identifiers: LCCN 2020029187 (print) | LCCN 2020029188 (ebook) | ISBN 9781644874028 (library binding) | ISBN 9781648342424 (paperback) | ISBN 9781648340796 (ebook)
Subjects: LCSH: Emergency medical technicians–Juvenile literature. | Emergency medicine–Juvenile literature.
Classification: LCC RC86.5 .M64 2021 (print) | LCC RC86.5 (ebook) | DDC 616.02/5–dc23
LC record available at https://lccn.loc.gov/2020029187
LC ebook record available at https://lccn.loc.gov/2020029188

Editor: Betsy Rathburn   Designer: Laura Sowers

Printed in the United States of America, North Mankato, MN.

Table of Contents

Saving the Day

Someone is hurt! The **ambulance** comes quickly. EMTs move the **patient**.

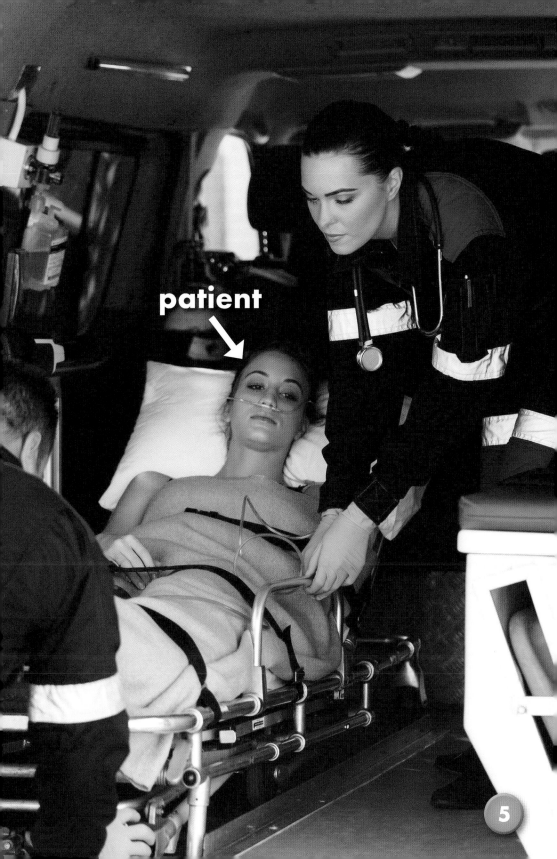

patient

The EMTs care
for the patient.
They are here
to help!

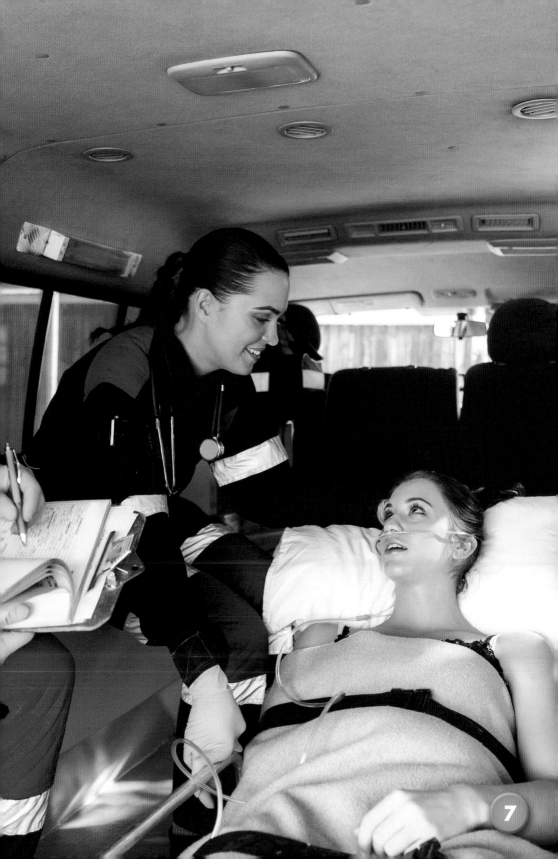

What Are EMTs?

EMTs are **emergency** medical technicians. EMTs take people to **hospitals** when they are sick or hurt.

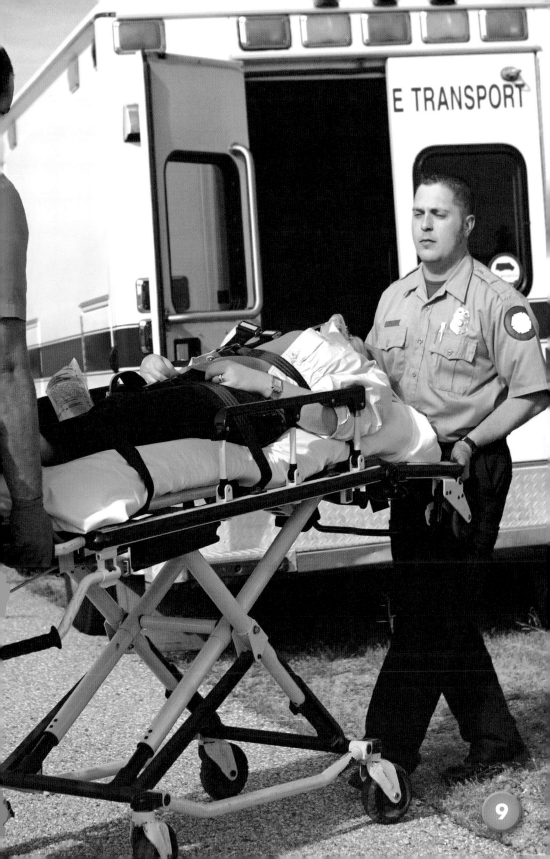

EMTs drive ambulances. They often work with police and firefighters.

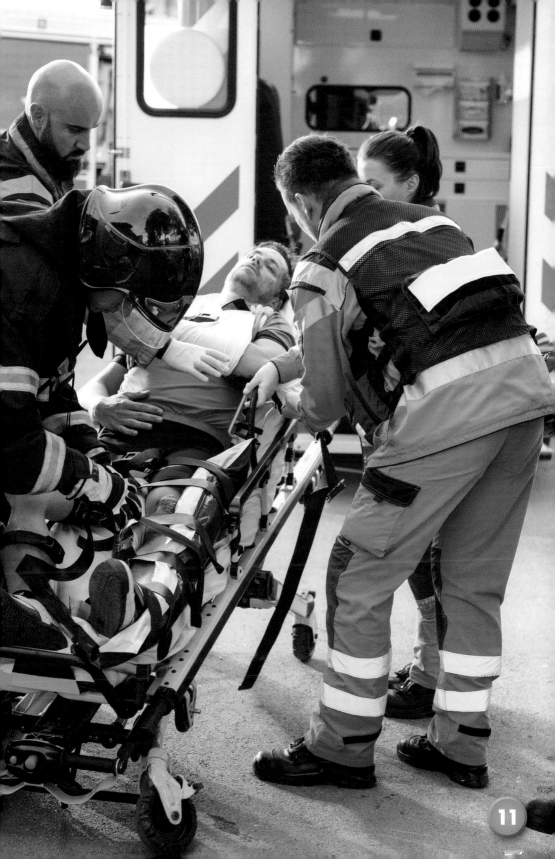

What Do EMTs Do?

EMTs find out what patients need.
They give **first aid**.
They give **CPR**.

EMTs write down what they know about patients. They share it with doctors and nurses.

EMTs make sure ambulances have supplies. They keep supplies clean.

EMT Gear

stethoscope   ambulance   stretcher   bandages

What Makes a Good EMT?

Emergencies can be scary. EMTs explain what is happening. They help people calm down.

EMT Skills

- ✓ good communicators
- ✓ good problem-solvers
- ✓ calm
- ✓ strong

EMTs fix problems. They make emergencies safer. EMTs save lives!

Glossary

ambulance

a vehicle used to take hurt or sick people to the hospital

first aid

emergency care for a hurt or sick person

CPR

a way of trying to save someone's life

hospitals

places where people receive emergency care or longer medical visits

emergency

an unexpected situation that calls for immediate attention

patient

a person in need of medical care

To Learn More

AT THE LIBRARY

Leaf, Christina. *Doctors*. Minneapolis, Minn.: Bellwether Media, 2018.

Manushkin, Fran. *Super Paramedic!* North Mankato, Minn.: Picture Window Books, 2020.

Zachary, Paul. *Ambulances*. Hallandale, Fla.: Mitchell Lane, 2019.

ON THE WEB

FACTSURFER

Factsurfer.com gives you a safe, fun way to find more information.

1. Go to www.factsurfer.com.

2. Enter "EMTs" into the search box and click 🔍.

3. Select your book cover to see a list of related content.

Index

The images in this book are reproduced through the courtesy of: Tyler Olson, front cover, pp. 18-19; michaeljung, pp. 4-5, 6-7; sirtravelalot, pp. 8-9; vm, pp. 10-11; Kzenon, pp. 12-13, 22 (emergency); Tony Tallec/ Alamy, pp. 14-15; kali9, pp. 16-17; JethroT, p. 17 (stethoscope); ravis manley, p. 17 (ambulance); Javier Crespo, p. 17 (stretcher); sumroeng chinnapan, p. 17 (bandages); FangXiaNuo, pp. 20-21; Christian Delbert, p. 22 ambulance); all_about_people, p. 22 (CPR); Leszek Glasner, p. 22 (first aid); Spotmatik Ltd, p. 22 (hospitals); Monkey Business Images, p. 22 (patient).